ANCIENT SKYSCRAPERS:

The Native American Pueblos

by
Sherry Paul

cpi
contemporary perspectives, inc.

This book is distributed by Silver Burdett Company, Morristown, New
Jersey, 07960.

Library of Congress Number: 78-23992

Art and Photo Credits

Cover photo, Jim Hileman
Photos on pages 13 and 37, Department of Development, Sante Fe,
    New Mexico
Photos on pages 16 and 25, Jim Hileman
All other photos in this book are by Sherry Olan.
Every effort has been made to trace the ownership of all copyrighted
material in this book and to obtain permission for its use.

Library of Congress Cataloging in Publication Data

Paul, Sherry
    Ancient skyscrapers: the native American Pueblos.

    SUMMARY: Highlights the history and way of life of the Pueblo
Indians.
    1. Pueblo Indians — Juvenile literature 2. Pueblos — Juvenile
literature. [1. Pueblo Indians. 2. Indians of North America] I. Title.
E99.P9P34   970'.004'97   78-23992
ISBN 0-89547-064-0

Manufactured in the United States of America
ISBN 0-89547-064-0

Contents

cover photo: Apartment houses built almost one thousand years ago, in Canyon de Chelly, Arizona, part of the Four Corners region.

Chapter 1
Around A.D. 1400 — Trouble on the Way

Spotted Deer was angry. But there was no one to be angry *at* except himself! Why had he not stayed at his post on the mountaintop? He should not have come down to hunt so early. If he had looked out to the plains before, he would have seen the group of men now moving toward him. He would have had another minute or so to warn the others.

The men moving quickly across the flat land were strangers to Spotted Deer. But he knew just why they were coming toward his mountain home. So would the rest of his people.

The only question now was — *could he warn his tribe in time?*

The morning sun was still low. Spotted Deer made for the shadows at the base of the mountain. He did not know if he had been seen yet.

He headed for a hidden path up the smooth, rocky face of the mountain. A last backward look told him there were about 25 of them — and they were still coming.

Spotted Deer began climbing. Up he went, quickly and surely. First the ladder and then the cliff itself. He knew this mountain well. His feet seemed to find each rocky step by themselves. With one hand he grabbed for higher rocks to pull himself along. His other hand held fast to the plant stem tied around the rabbits and prairie dogs he had caught for the day's food.

Halfway to the top, Spotted Deer looked back. The men had reached the shadows below. He watched to see where they would climb.

Good! They had not followed him. They had picked the long way up the mountain. That gave him more time!

Spotted Deer reached the light-colored rock near the top. He looked along the two miles of cave openings. Many of these caves were empty. Most of the people who had lived in them were now in the houses above. These houses were called *pueblos* (PWAY-blowz). They were tall apartment houses built on the *mesa* — the flat mountaintop. Spotted Deer's people, too, were known as Pueblos.

It was good that the people had moved to the pueblo, Spotted Deer thought. Pueblo families lived together in many rooms that rose high above the ground. They were safer from attack. They could lock out strangers like the raiders now climbing the mountain.

But a few of the older people in the tribe were still living in the caves. They wanted to keep the old way of life. Spotted Deer ran to the cave of Morning Bird. "*Apachu* [our enemies] are coming!" the young man yelled. "Up the side of the mountain away from the Great River!" Spotted Deer's strong arm pointed west, away from the Rio Grande.

The old cave homes were cut into the mountainside. Spotted Deer made for the ladder that would take him halfway to the mesa.

Morning Bird began to hit the cave wall with a rock. He was thumping a warning call to those in the other caves.

Spotted Deer climbed onto the top ledge of rock. He threw his day's food over and then pulled himself up to the flat mesa.

The rest of the tribe was awake. Dark streams rose from the smoke holes of the pueblo rooms. All the wood ladders were down. They leaned against the roofs of the two- and three-story pueblo. The ladders were used to get in and out of the apartment house. There were no openings on the ground floor.

In times of trouble, the ladders were pulled up to the lowest roof so no unwanted person could enter the first-story rooms through openings in the roof.

Spotted Deer ran through the chilly morning air. He headed straight for the *kiva* — a round, stone-walled underground room. Every Pueblo tribe had at least one such kiva. The men held their important business and religious meetings there.

Spotted Deer reached the ladder that poked up through the kiva opening. Climbing down into the darkness, he found the war chief and his hunting leaders. The chief had long ago proven his courage by bringing to his people the scalp of an apachu.

8

Spotted Deer knew he had to warn the chief before his own wife and child. His first duty was always to the tribe.

He waited until one of the older men spoke to him. These older men of the tribe came from two groups, called *moieties* (MOY-uh-teez). Each Pueblo tribe still has two such groups. They were like friendly clubs at times. At other times they were teams in games. The moieties were also like political parties in the Pueblo government. At Spotted Deer's pueblo one was the Summer moiety, and the other was the Winter moiety.

"There are many men climbing the mountain, sir," said Spotted Deer to the tribal elder. "They are

Spotted Deer climbed down the ladder into the kiva. Almost 10,000 years before Columbus, the Pueblo people used underground rooms like this as their homes. Knowing this, can we really say that Columbus discovered North America?

apachu — from across the flatlands toward the evening sun! They come with ugly weapons to steal our food and clay baskets." Spotted Deer was trying to catch his breath as his hand pointed to the southwest — the area that is now Arizona.

Quickly, the older men covered the flames in the fire pit in the center of the earth floor. They also made sure the *sipapu* was covered. The sipapu was a hole in the floor of the kiva. The Pueblo people believed their earliest grandparents came upon the earth through this hole.

Then, one by one, each man climbed the ladder. Spotted Deer, the youngest man, was the last to leave. From the kiva he ran to his own rooms in the pueblo.

The ruins of an ancient kiva. Religion is life itself to the Pueblo people. Their secret religious ceremonies are still held in the pueblo kivas.

What is left today of Spotted Deer's pueblo on the mesa at Puye, New Mexico. The walls were cut from the soft stone (tuff) of the mountain. Some two-story apartments have been rebuilt.

Now the women were all carrying children and food up the ladders. The men followed them to the rooftop openings. The older men and the women then pulled up the ladders and laid them on the roofs.

Spotted Deer ran out along the roof — thick tree branches that were placed across the walls and filled in with mud. He and the other men gathered together their bows and their largest stone arrows.

The younger men, armed and ready, spread out and hid behind rocks and the pueblo walls. They could do little to help any of their tribe still in the caves, but the *apachu* would not find it easy to attack the tall apartment house itself.

A roof at the Puye Pueblo. Young trees and branches were laid across wood poles that stuck through the stone walls. Space between branches was filled with mud.

No one made a sound inside the pueblo. Everyone knew an attack was just moments away.

Spotted Deer crouched low behind the far wall of the pueblo. There would be little sense in trying to stop the *apachu* before they came over the mountain ledge. They might be hidden by rocks. They might also duck into empty caves in the side of the mountain. No one would know where they were or how long they would stay hidden.

It would be better to stay here, behind the pueblo wall. Spotted Deer would be able to spot the first

12

apachu to climb up. He signalled to the others to wait until he gave the word.

Then he sat and waited. He thought about his wife and child inside the dark rooms on the other side of the wall.

Spotted Deer felt his hands shaking. He had good reason to be afraid. The *apachu* were big. His own people were not. Most were under five feet tall. Spotted Deer wondered if there would ever be a time when the outsiders would leave his people alone. It did not seem possible.

We are men who must fight even while we want to live in peace, thought Spotted Deer. Even while we hate to fight!

Pueblo women made fiber cooking baskets so tightly woven they carried water. By A.D. 900, they had learned to bake clay pottery for cooking.

Chapter 2

300 Years before Spotted Deer

Spotted Deer thought about the Pueblo past. He knew it well. His people had no books, but he had heard the stories told by his parents and others since he was a small child. It was only through stories that the people of a tribe knew their past, their laws, their religion. Nothing had ever been written down. No one had ever made up a way to write his tribe's *Tewa* language.

Spotted Deer's tribe — the people who now lived in "the home place of the eagle" — was peace-loving. All

The Pueblo dances tell stories of the past. Their history has never been written down.

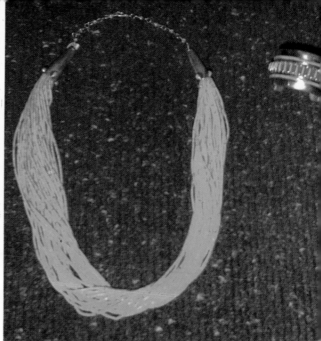

A modern wedding vessel from the San Ildefonso Pueblo and turquoise jewelry from the Zuni Pueblo. As the ancient Pueblo women had made their baskets, they had learned to sun-dry mud and form clay pots by about the year 900.

the Pueblo tribes were. They lived in villages strung out along the Rio Grande. Their apartment houses, many stories high, were the earliest "skyscrapers" in North America.

The Pueblo people worked as their ancestors had for thousands of years before them. The men used looms to make special clothes for religious dances and ceremonies. The women baked clay pots — just as their great-great-great-grandmothers had made tightly woven baskets for cooking and carrying water.

They farmed and fished and hunted. They picked wild berries and piñon nuts. They gathered seeds from the plains that stretched out below their mountains.

15

In search of water, the Pueblo people left their apartment houses in Canyon de Chelly, Arizona and the Four Corners area, and moved toward the Rio Grande in New Mexico.

But they never made war. A Pueblo tribe never fought with another Pueblo tribe. Nor would the Pueblo people ever go to war with anyone who left them alone.

The tribes in the mountains where Spotted Deer lived had come from the flatlands farther north and west. It was not far from where the four states we call Utah, Colorado, Arizona, and New Mexico meet. The tribes had left in search of better farmlands and safety from the weather — and from enemy tribes.

These enemies were the wanderers — the tribes that never raised their own food and had no lasting homes.

By around the year 1300 the Pueblo people and their enemies shared one problem. Their lands were dry. There had not been rain for almost 25 years. Hunting had become impossible. Animals died off or left the area in search of food and water.

But now, more than 100 years later, there were Pueblos living all along the rich Rio Grande Valley. Spotted Deer's home was in the area known today as Puye (POO-yay). It was not far from Bandelier Monument, one of the most beautiful national parks in modern North America.

To the south another tribe had built a much larger pueblo at Tyuonyi (chew-YO-nee) — "the meeting place." The Tyuonyi Pueblo had more than 400 rooms. Many of the houses were three stories high.

Like Spotted Deer's pueblo at Puye, the lower rooms of the Tyuonyi Pueblo were not lived in. There were no fireplaces in these rooms, since the smoke would have filled the rooms upstairs. They were used to store food, baskets, and other supplies.

The upper-floor rooms had fireplaces and smoke

holes. These were the sleeping and eating rooms that had to be kept warm during the cold seasons.

Tyuonyi was like a small fort-city. The pueblo was a closed circle with only one opening into the central plaza. In this opening, pointed wood stakes were planted in the ground. They would make it harder for enemies to enter. A large kiva was dug in the central plaza.

Some of the tribe did not want to live in the circle of rooms at Tyuonyi. Instead they built their homes against the bottom of the high cliffs that surrounded the pueblo. But others wanted their homes even higher. They found caves in the rock walls and lived more in the way their grandparents had lived.

The cave homes stretched out along the mountain wall. They were scooped out with stone tools. Walls and floors were plastered with mud. More than five people would usually share one cave room. The front wall had holes to get rid of the smoke that rose from the fire pit in the cave floor. There were no chimneys. Soot from the fire rose and blackened the ceiling.

The people in the Tyuonyi caves built their own cave kivas. Wood poles across the kivas held looms where the men did their weaving. It was usually the

Tyuonyi Pueblo was a circle of apartment houses around an open a. The round kiva (lower left) sat in the plaza. Tyuonyi lasted from ut A.D. 1100 until 1550.

One of the many cave homes in the cliffs overlooking Tyuonyi.

women of the village who did most of the home building. And good, strong homes they were.

The Pueblo tribes here also built skyscrapers. They were made of *tuff* — volcanic ash that had been pressed into mountain stone. Other tribes were

oking down at Tyuonyi were cliff houses like this *Talus House* (a house lt on fallen rock) on the Pajarito Plateau.

An ancient cave home near the Tyuonyi Pueblo (Bandelier National Monument, New Mexico). The Pueblo people carved pictures that told stories. These pictures, carved in the blackened rock, are called *petroglyphs*.

building their apartment houses of mud — called *adobe* (a-DOH-bee) — or of sandstone, for hundreds of miles along the Rio Grande.

Now, in the early 1400s, the Pueblo people lived in good homes. They were protected by the high mountains from the cold weather and from their enemies. On their new farms they grew the food they

The Great Cave Kiva near Tyuonyi, looking up from the Frijoles (Be Canyon.

needed. They planted corn, squash, and beans. They also learned to grow cotton with which they weaved strong cloth. From the stout fibers of the yucca plant they made sandals.

They had water from the Rio Grande. They trapped animals — gophers, prairie dogs, rabbits, deer, and mountain lion — for food. They fished with nets made from the hair of the women.

But they had their old enemies too, the *apachu* — later known as the Sioux, Apache, Navajo, Shoshone, Kiowa, and Cheyenne. These wandering tribes called themselves *Dine* — the people. They grew no food, raised no cotton, made no pottery, wove no cloth. Whenever hunting became hard for them, they raided the Pueblos. They carried out these attacks for more than 700 years.

And now, on a sunny morning in 1424, a party of *apachu* was creeping up on the Puye pueblo where Spotted Deer and his tribe lived.

To the valleys of the Rio Grande came the Pueblo people. They came in search of good soil for their farms, high mountains for their apartment houses, and safety from outsiders. They found their farmlands, and they built their tall apartment houses. But would the outsiders ever leave them in peace?

A modern-day colored clay bowl from the San Ildefonso Pueblo.

 ## Chapter 3
An Apachu Raid

Some of the *apachu* spread out over the rock ledge just under the pueblo. Others climbed across rocks to the cave openings under the ledge. It was hard going for the small prize they would win. Most of the cave homes were empty.

But the *apachu* did get some grain and seeds from a few of the caves. From the wife of old Morning Bird, they stole beautiful clay pots. When Morning Bird tried to take the pots back, the raiders killed the old man and woman.

Shrieking their war cries, the *apachu* now climbed over the ledge. But the first attacker fell back down the steep slope as Spotted Deer's silent arrow whizzed through the air and found its mark. That was the signal the Pueblo men had been waiting for!

From behind the pueblo walls and from rocks to the sides, arrows flew at the stunned *apachu*. The attackers fanned out and turned their stone axes against the Pueblo men. The *apachu* liked hand-to-hand fighting. The strongest of the Pueblo people hated fighting of any kind. And they did not train for war as the *apachu* did.

Pueblo arrows struck down two more of the enemy. But Spotted Deer's uncle did not hear one of the raider's footsteps behind him until it was too late.

A group of different stone arrowheads and an ancient hammering stone.

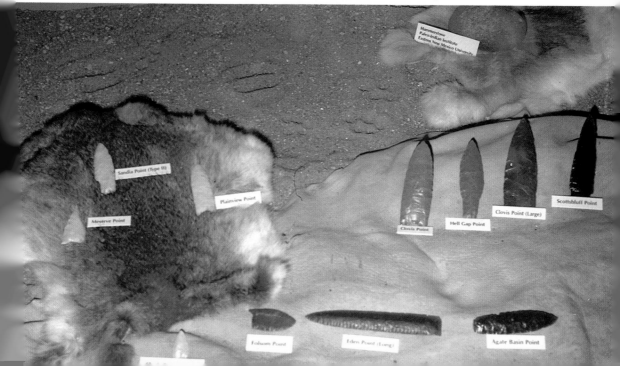

Spotted Deer saw but he was too far away to help. His arrow missed as the warrior's stone axe fell upon the head of Spotted Deer's uncle.

Without a sound, the murderer now climbed the wall of the pueblo and reached the first-floor roof. He ran toward the pueblo entrance and the frightened people inside.

Spotted Deer saw this too, but for the moment he could do little. One of the bigger *apachu* stood between him and the pueblo. The man was huge. Spotted Deer could not see any hope of winning a fight. There was no time for a bow and arrow. His only chance was to outsmart his enemy.

Still facing the man, Spotted Deer slowly backed away. The big *apachu* moved toward him but not too quickly. He too was being very careful. Spotted Deer was trying to lead him toward a side of the mesa where high weeds grew. There, hidden by the brush and weeds, was a pile of loom poles — and a steep drop off the mountain.

Suddenly Spotted Deer turned and ran toward the bushes. He reached the pile of long wood poles with his enemy about 30 feet behind. But to Spotted Deer it seemed as if the big *apachu*'s hot breath was racing across his own back.

Now Spotted Deer stopped running. He reached into the tall weeds and grabbed a long loom pole with both hands. With all his strength, he swung the pole in a circle — first away from the surprised enemy and then around and toward his back.

The pole struck the *apachu* just as he tried to turn and get away. Hitting him in the side, the force of the heavy pole drove him forward into the brush and weeds — and over the hidden cliffside.

Still shaking, Spotted Deer ran back to the pueblo. He jumped high to reach the top of the wall and held fast, scraping up the side with his feet until he was on the roof. The *apachu* who killed his uncle was inside the pueblo. *He had to get him out!*

Spotted Deer heard noise coming from the second-floor rooms to his right. He ran quickly across the clay floors, from one room to the next, until he saw the reason for the noise. Several of the women had the *apachu* on the floor! One was Spotted Deer's wife, Little Bird.

The women were clubbing the *apachu* with heavy clay pots, sleeping mats, anything they could swing. They turned when Spotted Deer entered the room.

But that gave the man on the floor a chance to get back on his feet!

The *apachu* pushed Spotted Deer aside and made for the rooftop opening. Spotted Deer followed quickly, almost catching the man before he jumped to the ground below. Off balance, Spotted Deer fell from the roof. The *apachu* turned back and picked up a rock that had come loose from the pueblo wall. He raised it high over Spotted Deer's head and brought it down hard.

The *apachu* then ran to join his brothers, who were climbing back down the mountain with the crumbs of food they had been able to steal.

Spotted Deer's body lay in the cool shadows of the pueblo wall. Little Bird and the other women began to lower the ladders from the roof. But the 18-year-old husband of Little Bird would climb the ladders of his beloved pueblo no more. Spotted Deer was dead.

The *apachu* picked up a loose stone from the pueblo wall and brought it down ... hard!

Chapter 4

300 Years after Spotted Deer

Leaping Waters had been listening to his uncle's stories of the past. He liked best the story of Spotted Deer, his ancestor who had lived in Puye — almost 300 years before.

Over the centuries the daughter of Spotted Deer, and all the daughters who followed, had married and moved to the pueblos of their husbands. This has always been the way of the Pueblo people. The children belong to the mother's family line (the clan). They are always members of her tribe, no matter where they live.

Now, in 1696, Leaping Waters was living in the pueblo of Taos. It was far north of Puye and Tyuonyi. Leaping Waters had been named for the clear rushing river that flowed through the center of Taos.

His pueblo was a series of apartment houses, from one to five stories high, made of adobe. Sandstone or tuff were not found this far north. Wood stakes and cross-poles were built as forms for the walls. Into these

The Taos Pueblo as it looks today. Leaping Waters was named for th small river that runs through the pueblo.

wood forms the adobe mud was poured. When the mud baked in the sun, the walls became hard clay.

The pueblo roofs were made from round young tree poles cemented together with mud. As in the other pueblos, there were no first-floor doors and ladders were used to climb to rooftop openings.

In the upper-floor rooms of the pueblo were the sleeping places. On the roofs were the beehive-shaped ovens the women used to bake their heavy corn bread. Near the pueblo was the round room and ladder of the kiva.

But now there was another religious place at the

pueblo. It was the Catholic church that had been brought by the Spanish — the first white people ever to visit the Pueblo people.

From the early 1400s Spanish explorers had been coming to the lands of present-day New Mexico. They were looking for "cities of gold" they had heard about in stories of the New World (North America).

But the first Spaniard to meet the Pueblo people was, as a matter of fact, not white at all. He was black. His name was *Esteban.*

In 1539 Esteban, a Spanish slave, left Mexico with Fray Marcos, a priest. They moved northward in search of a fairy tale — the "Seven Cities of Cibola" — seven cities of gold. The Spanish had heard that these cities had houses reaching up ten or more stories into the air. The people who lived there, Esteban thought, must have wings. *How else could they live so high from the ground?*

Fray Marcos agreed. *Of course, that must be it! These were the magic cities, the Seven Cities of Cibola. Did the people not have wings to fly to their homes in the air?*

With no stone for building, the Taos Pueblo was built with smooth adob walls that rose five stories into the air.

Esteban had moved ahead as a scout. With him was a small group of Mexicans. Fray Marcos was following, many days behind. When the priest reached the land that is now Arizona he met people who laughed at the idea of magic cities where people fly. *They use ladders,* the priest was told. *That is how they climb to the highest floors.*

Esteban never returned. One of the Mexicans who had gone ahead with him came back to Fray Marcos with bad news. Esteban had indeed found one of the cities. But he frightened the people there with his harsh demands and they had him put to death.

Fray Marcos dared to go on. From a far-off hill he saw the city of skyscrapers. But he would go no further.

Today the bake ovens can be safely used on the ground. With no fear of enemy attacks, there are doors at the ground level. Ladders are still used to climb to the upper floors of the apartment houses.

Fray Marcos went back to Mexico. He told the Spanish what he had seen. *The city sat on a flat plain at the base of a hill. There were houses made of stone reaching into the air for many stories. They had flat roofs.*

What about the gold, he was asked. *No, he had seen no gold, but he had heard that there was much of it in the city.* That was enough for the Spanish to hear. A city of stone skyscrapers and gold everywhere!

In 1540 they sent a 30-year-old adventurer, Francisco Vasquez de Coronado, northward to find the Seven Cities. He left with hundreds of soldiers and thousands of horses to claim the golden cities for his king. With him was the priest, Fray Marcos.

Two men of Taos live and work today...

Coronado's army never found the gold, but they did find the Pueblo skyscrapers.

They also found the peace-loving, hard-working Pueblo people. They watched the farmers till their fields. And they looked in wonder at the great amount of corn the women ground on sandstone slabs. The women ground in time to music played for them on flutes by the men.

... much as their ancestors of long ago.

And the hungry Spanish army stole food from these people.

Coronado's men attacked the Pueblos of the Zuni tribe of Arizona. They next went to war against the Hopi Pueblos. The Pueblos were frightened by the metal weapons of the Spanish. But most of all they feared the horses the Spanish rode. They had never before seen the "animals that eat people."

For the next 50 years the Spanish moved farther and farther north — as far as the Rio Grande — into the land that is now New Mexico. They brought a new religion they hoped would replace the old religion of the Pueblo people. They built Spanish churches alongside the Pueblo kivas. The names of the Pueblo people became Spanish names.

And the Pueblo people became Spanish slaves.

Those who had built the first skyscrapers—the earliest apartment houses—were now ruled by the Spanish government. And so they would be for more than 100 years.

This was the story Leaping Waters had heard from his uncle. This was the story he was remembering as he waited now for the Spanish to attack.

The year was 1696, and the people of Taos Pueblo were fighting to rid themselves of Spanish rule. They had fought their harsh rulers many times in the past. They hoped this time would be the last.

But like Spotted Deer, his grandfather of old, Leaping Waters could not believe his people would ever know peace.

Chapter 5

June 4, 1696 – The Spanish Are Coming!

Leaping Waters watched as the last of the ladders was pulled up to the roof of the pueblo. He and the other men of Taos were fanned out around the pueblo and at the back of the Spanish church.

Some of the men also hid just behind the riverbank. They would be the first to see the Spanish soldiers who would attack from the plains. This was where Leaping Waters lay, watching the first rays of sun glowing on the mountains.

Leaping Waters could not stop thinking of his uncle's stories. Just 21 years ago, the young man had heard, the Spanish hanged or whipped dozens of Pueblo people at San Ildefonso. The Pueblo people had been found guilty of witchcraft.

One of the Pueblo men whipped was Popé of Taos.

Walls are often built around the modern-day kivas to keep the secrets of Pueblo religion safe. Near this kiva at San Ildefonso Pueblo ...

He later led the war of 1680 when the Spanish were thrown out.

The Apaches fought the Spanish everywhere too. But they did not care that they also destroyed the pueblos near the Spanish villages. Leaping Waters's people all along the Rio Grande lived in fear of both the Spanish and the Apaches.

In Leaping Waters's pueblo the people had been

… stands the Catholic church, a sign of the Spanish entry into the lives of the Pueblo people.

rising against their rulers since as far back as 1632 and had even forced them to leave several times. But the Spanish always returned. *Could this time be different? Would his children be safe after today?* These were Leaping Waters's last thoughts before the first wave of Spanish troops attacked Taos.

By the end of the morning scores of Taos men lay dead in the village. They had cut down many soldiers, but the odds against the Pueblo people were too great.

43

The first defenders of the pueblo to die were the men fighting at the river. Leaping Waters did not live to see his own wife and children flee west to the Hopi lands of Arizona.

Some animal-hide clothing of the Pueblos, with a baby's cradle and fur blanket.

Chapter 6

The
 **Acoma Pueblo**
– Nearly
300 Years Later

Victor Correro sat high on the cliff that rose above the plains around his pueblo in southwestern New Mexico. His eyes took in the sparkling sunlit mountains and shimmering rooftops of the "sky city" that was his village of Acoma. Below, Route 23 stretched out like a dark ribbon toward Albuquerque.

It was a religious day for the Pueblos. The older men of the tribe were already meeting in the kiva. On such days only members of the tribe could be in Acoma.

Victor now had the job of watching for any strangers who might try to enter the pueblo. He would have to turn them away.

Victor was sleepy this morning. He had been up late last night, listening again to the stories of his people and his own clan. He loved the stories of his ancient grandfathers, Spotted Deer and Leaping Waters. He never missed the chance to hear of their children and the marriages that had brought his family to Acoma.

Suddenly Victor's sleepy eyes opened wide. A light-colored car was making its way along Route 23 toward the steep, unpaved cliff road that climbed up to the Acoma pueblo.

Pulling himself to the top of the highest rock, Victor waved his mirror. The sunlight leaped from the shiny glass to a spot below where another young man sat.

All the Pueblo stories now came to Victor's mind. All he could think about was the years of fighting for their skyscraper villages and a peaceful life. Even now the modern-day grandson of the first apartment-house builders was watching for unwanted strangers who would try to enter the Pueblo world.

The young man below waved the car to a stop.

Acoma, the "sky city," was built on top of a cliff 357 feet over the plains small number of families still live in the Pueblo apartment houses with running water or electricity.

Victor smiled as he watched the strangers turn around and head back to Albuquerque.

Still smiling, Victor looked to the sky. His thoughts were spoken to the white cloud puffs that hung just above his head:

"No, my grandfathers, the outsiders will never leave us alone. But perhaps that is best. We must still fight to keep our way of life. But the battle is no longer bloody. We have our Pueblo world and we share the world outside with others. The best of both worlds is what we wish for people everywhere."